THIRD EYE AWAKENING V

Therone Shellman

Authors Notes

Everyone possesses some level of psyche and intuition, and some more than others. Nevertheless, to grow in the skill requires conscious work just like developing any other skill or talent.

ISBN: 9798366212823
ISBN: 8366212823

Published by Therone Shellman Media
Edited by BlackInk
Proofread: Therone Shellman Media

CONTENTS

INTRODUCTION

As the saying goes 'seek knowledge from the cradle to the grave.' There's also another saying which states 'your life will prepare you for your purpose.' My life struggles have been my greatest strengths and motivation. As a child I realized that people in general couldn't be counted on to do the right thing unless they were forced to. I couldn't wait to grow up and become an adult so I could be responsible for myself. Now as a 51-year-old I realize that I can always depend on me no matter what. I've fallen many times and each time I've picked myself back up, licked my wounds and done what's necessary. When there are things to learn I take to task to study, and when there are things to do, I always manage to do them. Knowledge is my friend and I realize that not knowing a knowledge which is important to my life is costly for I have paid the cost many times.

We're with ourselves throughout our whole lifetime. 'Wherever you go there you are' and it's such a true quote and statement. For some reason I've never sought to run from myself and instead have sought to figure out what makes me tick, and what is it that I'm tasked to do in the world in relation to interests, natural skills and abilities. In seeking to understand myself I stumbled upon the power of vision and visualization and the reality that humans have a level of existence which is greater than mind. Realization is the key. The mind is a tool and we can wield power over it just like a flashlight, or movie screen projector. I'm learning to think higher and broader, and this work is a look into the many experiences that intuition and psyche have played in my life. Like a child I've stumbled on many occasions. The world is always teaching, and every now and then I'm reminded that we're actually in school all day and if we fail to take heed to signs, warnings, visions, and whispers we'll fail tests and pay the penalty. The main test for all of us is to trust ourselves, and our abilities.

I'm excited about this work as I enter a new era in my life, one which is about the work. I've tested my knowledge, I'm capable, skilled and able to do whatever I task to. Now I'm at the doorway and ready to enter a phase of my life which is all about the work, and I have many tasks. Some of

which I share in this book, and others
which are only for my knowing.

Everyone I've encountered in transaction of
experiences and energy has helped me in
some way or another. Whether it was
pleasant or unpleasant I've learned to
evaluate situations as they apply to my
life. Time and effort are priceless so it's
important to learn to avoid the unneces-
sary, take advantage of fruitful opportunities, handle situations accordingly and
deal with people according to the manner
the encounter and the person needs to be
dealt with.

I believe that we're far much greater than
we can imagine or the powers that be have
revealed. I used to think we were a sum of
our mind but life has shown me that we're
greater than mind and thought and wield
power over both. We've traded AI-artificial
intelligence for human intelligence. We've
been tricked into believing that technology
is our savior and will make our lives a
whole lot easier and fulfilling. It's created a
bunch of confusion, uneasiness and lazy
people. No one wants to think for themselves, and so they've turned over the
power of thought to the most intellectual
and so this group being more intelligent

than most of the masses has created technology smarter than the majority of humans. This is a huge problem now and will
become an even greater threat in years to
come. Intelligence grows in intelligence
and so what happens if or when such intelligence decides it doesn't need humans to
think? The only alternative is to urge humans to return to a state of thinking where
learning and creativity are worthy skills
and endeavors. We have the ability to see
beyond our learning and physical sight
and so the Third Eye Awakening series of
books are here to aide in becoming a more
complete being and thinker.

Third Eye Awakening V 'Psychic Intuition'

psy·chic
/ˈsīkik/
adjective

1.
relating to or denoting faculties or phe-
nomena that are apparently inexplicable
by natural laws, especially involving telep-
athy or clairvoyance.
"psychic powers"

in·tu·i·tion
/ˌint(y)oōˈiSH(ə)n/
noun

the ability to understand something immediately, without the need for conscious
reasoning.
"we shall allow our intuition to guide us"

Sometimes the World Knows Who You Are Before You Do.

"Sometimes You Know What You Don't Know"

Arriving to half a decade of consciousness, has provided me with enough insight and experience to draw from and realize what Knowledge of Self truly is. It's more than the acknowledgment of race, culture and even species. It's the understanding of knowing biologically what makes us who we are as a species, and also as individual creations within the sphere of all life creations. The more Intune we are with ourselves, the more aware we are of our individual powers, senses and insights. After all we are the embodiment of consciousness. At the age of seventeen I would encounter a situation which would change my life forever, and at the same time bring me into the awareness of a power I possessed. The most unfortunate thing is that I didn't recognize it then as a power, and for many years just went on with my life not recognizing the gift I possessed.

I had a dream where I see myself walking through a path everyone utilized to cut through a wooded area to get to the next block. The path was linked to an area of woods connected to the high school yard. While walking I heard my name being called. "Therone, Therone is that you?" I don't remember the exact words because, it's been so long. Yet, I do remember my name being called out. I remember it as if it was yesterday. Hesitantly I turned around to look, and there was a tall Caucasian man with a gun and a badge held in his right hand. He held out the badge so I could see it, mentioning he was a detective. Long story short, the next day I ended up being arrested. I dreamt the whole situation the night before.

For the next few days in my cell I thought about how I dreamt the whole situation. Quickly I forgot because, I was forced to deal with the reality of my present life of being incarcerated and facing some years. The next time I would be revisited by such sight and psyche again would be when I was around 22 years old."

"Once Is a Coincidence. But When You Find Yourself Being Shown Situations Visually Before Their Physical Occurrence More Than

Once. It's No Longer a Coincidence."

Okay, so now I'm 22 years old just released from prison about six months earlier after serving 4 ½ years. While incarcerated I wasn't too concerned with sports and hanging out. I spent most of my time studying. Whether, it was reading history, self-help books, law books, or amongst my 5 Percent brothers talking about social issues, and our lessons. I also spent a lot of time reading business books. I would get how-to pamphlets from the business administration on different business skills and industries mailed to me. Let's just say that when I was released there were many things running through my mind. But the most important was getting myself together financially It's 1994, I was just released from prison, and have a Class B Felony. Honestly, it would be easier for me to get some drugs to sell, than obtain a decent paying job. This is the reality I was faced with. After weighing my options for a few weeks, I made the decision to take my ambition to the streets. It took me a few weeks after the decision, but I was able to scrape together about $100 to

begin my street pharmacy venture to pur-
chase 3 grams of crack/cocaine (base.)

I flipped the $100 package to about $170,
and kept doing this until I was able to pur-
chase 28 grams (1 ounce.) This took me
about two weeks to get to the point where
I had $800. Believe it or not this wasn't an
easy endeavor because, like with any other
product and sales it's all about building a
customer base. When no one knows you,
it's all about building trust. Trust in you,
and trust in your product. One of the
houses I posted up at night and sold
product at also happened to be where the
girlfriend of one of my customers stayed
at. He comes to me one day and lets me
know the guy down the street who runs a
spot wants to talk to me about coming
down there too and hustling at the spot.
So I go down there, and the hustler and I
strike a deal to split the spot. Everything is
going great for about a month. Yet, I begin
to get bad vibes. Somethings telling me to
be very cautious, and alert. In other words
Keep All 3 Eyes Open.

Over the next few weeks some events
transpire which let me know that I may of
stepped into a burning house, and maybe I
should just back out. By this time though,

and just that quick I was now grossing around $10,000 plus a week. Being young and greatly influenced by money my vision was clouded. Now almost three decades later I overstand the power of intuition, and the importance of paying attention to first thought, and the eerie feeling one gets in their gut. To also move in the right way when you're shown unfavorable situations.

To make a long story short our drug spot was raided, and from intel I was told I was set up with the intention of targeting me. So in other words I was to be sacrificed. If I had not paid attention to my intuition to be on point I would of gotten caught up. Instead as the police surrounded the blocks and started to rush the house, I jumped in track star mode and ran like my life depended on it. It was like being in a movie. As I'm running through yards I see police grabbing, and tackling guys. Three blocks away I hid within a wooded area, and within minutes I seen someone I know and called out to them. Crawling to their car I got in ducked down while they took me home. My adrenaline was so pumped that I actually wasted not one second of thinking of fear. When I reached safety I was actually in disbelief in how I got away.

There was no time for much thinking. I just moved, and moved in a manner of perfection that I believe was divinely carried out to get me out of danger because, had I gotten caught surely, I was going back to prison. To make matters worse the whole time I had a gun, and a large sum of drugs on me." I was definitely going to go down for a long time that was certain. Fate was on my side because the best possible outcome came my way. Not listening to myself and backing out of the situation could of cost me my life. Being on point though allowed me to see the situation formulate when it did and make the necessary adjustment in action. Lucky me.

"Like a Mathematical Equation, Everything Appears In Patterns. It's All a Puzzle That One Must Decipher and Put Together"

Sometimes, it's necessary to sit back and evaluate your vision with a second, third, and fourth look. When you're dealing with people behavior is a powerful and truthful yardstick to measure by. Most people are creatures of habit, and tend to do the same routine frequently. Therefore, when someone deviates from a pattern pay attention because, it's a good chance somethings out of whack. Taking all of this into account is probably why I got out of this situation a free man. I realized that my business partner made a few moves that just didn't add up that morning. This automatically put me on alert, even if I couldn't put my eye on what exactly had me at unease I knew just to be on point without knowing what to be on point about. While everyone else was playing dice, goofing off and not paying attention I was standing, alert and at attention. So when a couple of neighborhood kids rode by on their bicycles screaming that the police were coming and about to raid I just started running without thinking about anything else. This is how I ended up getting away.

A few days after the event I decided to go see me partner, to let him know my thoughts about the situation, and that our business association had come to the end. By the way his code name is EJ. This is the same name I gave him in Survivor I Changed the Rules my autobiography. Those familiar with me, and my street activities at the time know who he is. From what I've learned he was placed in a federal witness protection program as a result of becoming a federal informant and setting up other drug dealers from the same neighborhood he was raised and grew up in. So now he's somewhere in a southern town with a new life living it up after setting up associates and people he's known his whole life. It's crazy how I saw this in him being an outsider about five years before he pulled his final act. I'm thankful that I did see it in him, got away, and decided to stay clear of him. Yet people who knew him his whole life or for many years didn't have a clue. I possibly could have really gotten caught up five years later had I not figured him out. Eyesight beyond physical site is so important. So is sticking to your gut feeling once you make a decision about people and situations. I made the decision to stay clear of him and I stuck with it.

"Pay Attention and Be Aware of Your Environment"

Situational awareness is one of the most important skills linked to nature that one can develop. One is driven to look beyond physical eyesight, see and feel with their senses. Envision with one's mind. Feel and hear the vibrations, and energy of others and the earth. Prison, urban neighborhoods, and warzones present great environments to develop this skill. The more one is free of substances and information (media) that lowers one's ability to think freely the quicker they'll be able to tap into and connect to their primitive instincts.

While on parole there were several times where I realized I was being followed. One time I was standing at a bus stop waiting, and something told me to look in the parking lot across the street. Immediately I see a Caucasian middle aged man with silver hair staring at me. When he notices I spotted him, he turns away. I didn't write it off as a casual coincidence because something about him put me on alert. About two weeks later while checking in with my parole officer at the office I notice the same guy walk in from the outside door. He said nothing to the other parole officers and proceeded to walk straight to one of the back offices. Parole investigator is the first thing which came to my mind. I was going to say something to my parole officer but then quickly decided against it. Now there were no doubts in my mind that I was under some sort of investigation.

There were a few parole officers who had it out for me. I knew I had to watch my back. I knew for sure that someone, or some people were setting things up behind the scenes. It's one thing to assume something. Yet it's a whole another situation when you walk right into a scene which validates your thoughts. I've only been released for about a month from the violation and I was sure that moves were being made to ensure that when I decide to make the wrong move someone would be there to spot it so they can violate my parole. To make matters worse other parolees were speaking my name to parole officers. At one of my check in visits my parole officer told me that someone was trying to throw me under the bus to take the spotlight off of them. One of those why are you messing with me? Why aren't you messing with such and such? It turns out the guy was like family to someone who I was beginning to get cool with.

About five weeks later I was arrested and violated parole. To make a long story short I was charged with felony possession of a controlled substance. The charge winded up being dropped down to a misdemeanor, and I received a one year parole violation. The crazy thing is that the morning of the arrest I was with one of my lady friends. The whole time we were lying in bed I was contemplating whether I should just stay in and do nothing. Being the hustler that I am I decide to make some calls, and get the day going even though I was having bad feelings. After making sure she got on her way to go home I take a shower, get dressed, make a few calls and package some product for the day.

While in transit to make a drop off I get bad vibes, and many things about the scenery just didn't seem right. My mind was telling me to forget the drop off, retreat and keep it moving. In fact I thought about stashing the package and coming back for it later. This is exactly what I should have done. The importance of reading your environment cannot be overstated. If something doesn't seem right, there's a greater chance than not something off. I didn't take heed and paid the price. It winded up being a two year parole violation along with a misdemeanor.

"Dreams Can Come True, and Sometimes Dreams Are a Depic-

tion of What's to Come, or the Possibility of What Can Be."

It's 1999 and I'm serving a one year parole violation. I go to the board two months before I'm to be released and they serve me another year. They didn't come out and say it but I could read in between the lines. I winded up getting around an A1 felony possession of an uncontrolled substance on the technicality of illegal search and seizure, and the charge was dropped down to a misdemeanor. The detectives wanted me to help them set someone up, and if I agreed they would allow me to walk right out the back door. I refused, and let them know it's not the game I play. So they locked me up. One thing I was taught as a teen is to be knowledgeable about the laws surrounding whatever you're dealing with. In other words one is at a disadvantage when they're ignorant. Since this is so I took the time to learn the laws surrounding drug sales, possession, possession of firearms, search and seizure, etc. To make a long story short the case was dropped down to a misdemeanor possession. Over the first year of being locked down for the parole violation I thought about something the detective mentioned.

He mentioned that they were put onto me by someone who knows me. At the time one of the young ladies I was dealing with her brother was facing a federal case. There were rumors that he was trying to set folks up to get out the case. I wasn't sure about him, but I was sure that someone with details about my movements did feed the detectives as to my activities because the set up was perfect. Day in and day out I thought intensely about my associations, and I realized that I couldn't really trust anyone. Yet, I also realize some things are orchestrated by spiritual forces at play. Receiving the extra year on top of the year I was serving actually turned out to be a blessing in disguise. Throughout the first year all I thought about was how I was getting out, and getting back to the money. Some of it was about getting money, and a part of it was revengeful thinking. Receiving the second year made me realize though that the consequences far outweighed the value of money to me. At this time I was now 27 years old, and have survived a total of 6 1/2 years of my life within prison, and still had one more year to go. The streets love no one, and morals and values aren't a high priority when most are faced with the reality of dealing with their own karma. They would rather usher someone else into the line of fire which was meant for them. Realizing this I began to have a change of heart as days within the second year progressed.

One Cannot Become More Than They Envision Themselves to Be

Whether time is real, or just an illusion is a matter of perception. Yet to exist is real, and you can spend this existence experiencing that which you desire to experience. Or one can be forced to interact amongst situations which are bitter to the heart and soul and be a slave to experience what external forces determine.

The second year of the violation I've experienced many dreams. One which stood out to me the most was of me doing a book signing in the streets of NY. I'm at table filled with books, and I'm holding a book within my hand with the cover flap open, pen in hand and having a conversation with a book reader. Another potential customer is browsing the books upon the table. I saw the dream a few weeks before I went to the parole board and was given the extra year. It was at this point that I realized there was a greater calling for me. Yet I was conflicted with how to go about it all, and how to make the necessary changes in my life. I conformed to the life of the streets so well that it had become my world. The money, the social status, hustle was so me that it just seemed normal to the people around me. It was evident that for the remaining year of the violation there was much to think about. I needed to make a drastic change. One which was going to disrupt every area of my life. I no longer could utilize my youth misfortunes as a reason to try to take shortcuts when I was now well aware that there's no shortcuts to progress, or the attainment of anything worthwhile. Everything is the result of a process, the right actions, and sacrifice. There's always an exchange. I had given up freely 7 1/2 years of my life, and I hadn't reached the age of thirty. There was much negatives to take from the situation. The flip side is that there's always things to learn from experiences and I was learning little by little the pluses.

Life is strange and perception is so important. In some ways sometimes the picture will seem more clearer looking from the outside in than from the inside looking around. During the original 4 1/2 yr sentence some of my vocational instructors, and even counselors would tell me that I would make a great leader. My influence amongst my peers was evident. Strangely my first parole officer gave me some advice mentioning that I should transfer my parole from Suffolk County to one of the boroughs in NYC and go to college for law, etc. He told me that if I remained in Long

Island I would not make it past 18 months without getting a parole violation.

Throughout the second year of the parole violation I had much to think on. I needed to make a drastic change. One which was going to disrupt every area of my life. I no longer could utilize the misfortunes of my youth as a reason to try to take short cuts when I was now more than aware there's no short Cuts to progress, or the attainment of anything worthwhile. Everything is the result of process, the right action, and sacrifice. There's always an exchange. I had given up freely 7 1/2 years of my life. There was much negatives to take from the situation. The flipside is there's always things to learn from experiences, and I was learning little by little.

Be Still & You'll See What You Need to See

Our reality is determined by the level of our consciousness. So our actions are determined by our thoughts. One cannot act greater than they think unless by accident.

Practice discernment and all that isn't said will be shown, and all that our two physical eyes don't see you'll visualize. A case of knowing what I don't know has been my life experience. I've walked into situations knowing what I never took the time to learn, and in many instances I've been ushered into learning what I needed to take part in. Most importantly I've also been nudged into situations which shown me a truth I was seeking. Understand that the foundation of my studies began through the Nation of Gods & Earths (5% Percent Nation.) So the term God mind was something I was familiar with. Yet it takes time for understanding to develop. You can possess a knowledge, but yet not be comfortable enough with it to fully under-stand. The Source is an energy life source possessing all intelligence. We as being conduits (circuits) are tapped in, and the more we develop in consciousness the more access to intelligence we have. I'm constantly growing and evolving in knowledge and understanding. In the pre-vious Third Eye Awakening books I utilize the term God, Supreme Consciousness, In-finite Consciousness, etc. Now at this point I see none of them terms as being sufficient so I will utilize Source. For me this is a better definition to describe where all consciousness comes from. In the previous books I also talk of material and non-material matter. The last two years I learned that there's no such thing as matter in a physical sense. Things appear to have a physical existence because of our level of consciousness. Which explains how ancient African and indigenous civilizations speak of being in contact with other entities from other universes. Without all this technology, and manufactured food they were vibrating on a higher frequency. So their eyesight was far greater than current humans. There are parallel universes and dimensions, and most humans have no eyesight into other dimensions which co-exist with the one they exist in.

In 2000 I'm released after serving the two year violation. I made the decision that with only one year left of parole that I was going to make a drastic life transition, and get a job. The first thing I decided to do was not be paroled back to my normal environment. This was a daring move but I got paroled to a half-way house in a neighborhood about 30 minutes away. Out of sight out of mind. If I was away from my hustling associates, and drug fiends (customers) then my mind wouldn't be drawn to such. Selling drugs is an addiction just as much as drug use is. The hustle, excitement, money and the life creates a high, and I knew I needed to separate myself. During the second year of my incarceration EJ who I no longer dealt with but he had found his way to start dealing with a few of my business associates turned federal informant. Isn't this interesting how I had him figured out better than people who knew him his whole life, and others who hustled with him for years. He winded up setting some individuals up, and going into witness protection. When I got news of this my first thought was the extra year they added on to my original one year parole violation possibly was a blessing because, I could have gotten caught up in the set up. Sometimes things happen to you that seem unfair, but in reality these situations are just moving you out the way of real harm.

I go into the halfway house, and about six weeks later landed a job. $8.00 an hour, $320 a week a complete downgrade from $1000-$2000 a day. But a smart man changes, and an ignorant man keeps doing the same thing expecting different results, as the saying goes. I was moving close to 30 years old, and so I knew it was now or never. The next four years I move methodically and strategically applying what was learned in the streets to the work world. It's 2004, and I'm now a production supervisor after starting at the first company in 2000 as a quality assurance inspector, and moving on to four other companies upgrading my skills and pay along the way.

Once I reached the level of production supervisor I realized I was ready to go to the next stage and complete a task which I had been meditating on the past decade. I began laying down the bricks to publish my first book. After researching I found out there was such a thing as vanity publishing services. This is when one hires a company to help them transform their manuscript into a finished book. Once I was ready the whole process took about 3 months after submitting the manuscript. 2003, and it seemed like an eternity since I started to write the first draft of Love Don't Live Here somewhere around 1991-1992. I received the 500 copies and was thrilled. Yet, after reading the book I realized there was so many errors. Even as a novice I knew that ignoring proofreading and depending on others was a huge mistake. I sold around 125 copies and discarded of the rest. Being honest with myself I accepted that I needed to go back to the drawing board, and get the book put together properly. I also needed to do a whole lot more research on the book publishing industry as a whole. From this moment I committed myself to study. 18 months later in 2005 I republished Love Don't Live Here, and within 6 months sold close to 5,000 copies. Meditating on my truth, and working towards it brought me through that experience. The whole process of working my way from one job to the next to get to where I wanted, and then the humble beginnings of starting the first draft of Love Don't Live Here while incarcerated as a teen. Being patient, to live and experience the other necessities of my life, while at the same time keeping the vision of publishing the book in my mind. To see these things come to life helped me to understand the workings of cause & effect, and the power of visualization. No longer a theory but a tested truth. It was at this point that I realized there was a greater calling for me. How I was able to come to the accomplishment was started with one night lying in bed and focusing my thoughts 100% on my literary endeavors. In this moment I realized that I was going to have to educate myself on the whole process of publishing, plus create a program which was only for me. The next 18 months this is exactly what I did.

Envision the Pieces on the Board Before a Move Is Even Made.

Be Mindful That Enemies Disguised As Friends Are More Plentiful Than True Friends

I was tricked in the worse manner when I found out that in the real world there's a thin line between the streets and business world. The same players, they just appear to be different. I really thought the Black book industry was going to be all about Black love. Yes, us against the White establishment and the ideas which have raped Black artists, and even forced some to go across seas to work. Better yet the same industry which is the reason why independent Black book stores is necessary. If they published more Black authors, and the Caucasian owned book stores carried more Black published books there would be no need for a Black book market. I quickly found out there's no Black love but instead the love of and for capital first. I got backstabbed so many times within the first year of publishing that I had no choice but to understand that business is business, and it doesn't matter whether it's in the streets, or in a corporate office. People are the same, and so the environment may require a different strategy to deal with them. Yet if one sets themselves up to be played, they'll surely get played because folks are always looking for a sucker to take advantage of.

Friendships Aren't What They Used to Be

The saying that "we're lucky to have one true friend throughout our lives" is one of the truest and hardest truths we'll have to accept. Growing up through foster care and understanding abandonment as a child inflicted me with the idea of being loyal even when it wasn't in my best interests. It wouldn't be until my late twenties where I began to think of myself as a first in relationships.

Well, let's go on a journey and I will tell you of one individual who I considered to be a friend and even a brother. A brother is deeper than the bond of blood kinship. Soldiers know of brotherhood. Those who share the same ideals and who have stood together through opposition know of brotherhood. In the streets brotherhood bonds are formed. Yes, this individual I considered a brother, and maybe there was a time when he considered me the same. Yet, fate sometimes destroys beautiful things like the waves of crashing water for many years against a shore. In the end this individual would try to sacrifice me to serve his best interests. In other words he strived to sacrifice me as an offering to the dark interests he was in business with within the law enforcement establishment. Had I not been the enlightened being I am I would have surely been a victim. An associate of ours forewarned me. Around 2001 I get a call one day from an associate. He didn't hesitate to tell me that I needed to watch myself because while he was in the precinct with his lawyer a detective told him that the mutual associate of ours was snitching. It turns out I knew the attorney of my associate, and I knew him to be a stand-up guy. He handled federal and state criminal convictions, and was someone whose name carried respect. Definitely not one of the let's take a plea deal type of attorney. Nor was he cheap. So for the detective to say this in front of him to my associate let me know it was definitely true. It now also dawned on me that our mutual associate in question was getting visits from detectives to his house. He told me about a month earlier that the detectives were trying to shake him down about something serious. Putting two and two together along with the phone call I now realized they broke him and he was now cooperating. In other words he was snitching, and had become a confidential informant. Months later I learned the so called perpetrators of the crime they were pressing him about winded up receiving many years.

Once you get in the bed with the devil, and make a deal it doesn't end there. The contract is for a lifetime, and you'll never get free. This is the workings of the dark power. Many are lured to serve their desires and wants in return for them sacrificing something (usually their morals, values, or the betrayal of the bond of someone who trusted them.) Many don't realize the fine print of the contract. I've always been one to pay attention to what many allow to slip past them, and so as an early teen I realized that getting in bed with law enforcement was symbolic to getting in bed with the devil. One will not just give information and walk away. Man up, woman up and handle what your footsteps get you into. The funny thing is that I always told this guy and my other associates to stay clear of interacting with the police. My motto has always been if one is living on the wrong side of the law. If one isn't getting locked up then they have no business talking to law enforcement unless they were being asked the basics of questioning. Even then to be careful because if you're not being arrested the police have no business asking certain questions.

So now that I was sure that my associate was a confidential informant I made sure not to place myself in any compromising situations or do anything with his knowledge that he could get me knocked off on the low. Anything I did with him, he would also have to implicate himself. The situation was very fragile and I handled it as such. I've known his family for years, and was one of his older cousins was a friend and business partner years earlier. He was now incarcerated and in dealing with and doing business with the family this is how I became cool with the younger cousin.

Years would go by and now it's around 2018 and I realized the link between this associate and law enforcement. It had become obvious to me because I was seeing some things out in the open that I just couldn't ignore. The kicker was that at this point I was sure that he was on to me being on to him. When people know you have knowledge about them that could destroy them the obvious defense in many instances is to create a lie about you so people are looking at you and not them. This is also a tactic to plant fear in the knower. They'll create this false narrative amongst their circle, and also have their circle promote it. The slick thing about this is they will not do this in the open. Instead they'll create the propaganda, spread it amongst the circle, and stand back as if they're innocent and someone else started it all. Then they'll strive to act like they're your biggest supporter, and true friend.

People that know me know my morals and values, and so I didn't care about the rumors. I just stayed on task. In fact I opened my eyes even wider, and paid attention even more. If he was truly aware that I was aware of his relationship with the police, and now the smear tactics he was definitely now desperate more than ever to get me out the way. I was no longer in the streets, and didn't have the pull that I used to have in this neighborhood. Yet he on the other hand had grown influential in the streets. The main reason being that his family, extended and immediate were residents of this neighborhood

(Bellport, NY) for several years. My first hand eyesight, and knowledge gained on the matter allowed me to see how intelligence is gathered, and how confidential informants along with law enforcement operate on the street and community level. In a forth coming book titled Street Knowledge I will be more detailed about the process.

Through my dialogue the matter may seem simple and easy going, but we're talking about several years in an atmosphere in which things could have gone terribly wrong. I really believed then and now years later this info would be useful and great for a book. I also wanted to understand the dynamics of the whole confidential informant program as it relates to minority and urban communities. Remember these guys are given immunity to commit crimes as long as they provide info on others and serve the interests of their law enforcement handlers. Most importantly it's important to understand that law enforcement as an institution is a criminal enterprise in itself. This is what's so hard to stomach, but yet it's very true and real. Always remember that the first police officers were slave catchers. Law enforcement as an institution was founded upon racist ideas. I believe we're made by our travels and circumstances and those of us with extra abilities are tested more than others so that we can develop in our talents and skills. Being a creative person my experiences have helped me develop the eyesight to communicate certain realities most people can't see but need to be aware of.

Not Every Opportunity Is the Right One for You

I received an email from the Texas Work-
force Commission in regards to them facil-
itating production line hiring opportunities
with Tesla. Starting pay would be $19.50
which I wasn't too thrilled with. Yet considering the mega sized organization Tesla
is I decided to pursue the opportunity, and
see where it leads. With my manufacturing
skills ability and willingness to learn new
things, leadership and life experience I
figured I could quickly move up if not in
production, then over to another department.

Tesla recruiting contacts me about a
month later and invites myself along with
other potential candidates to a private
online interview session. I accept and at-
tend, and after send an email over to recruiting about my continued interest. Within the hour I receive a phone call and a
contingent offer dependent upon results
of drug screen and background check.

The next stage was setting up a drug
screen urine analysis date. Which I set for
the next day. While setting up the drug
screen I signed permission for the company Tesla works with to run a background
check. So I go and give the urine knowing
that I'm clean because, I don't utilize

drugs. 4 days later I receive a call from Tesla recruiting in regards to my urine sample being cleared. The next step is to wait for the background check. The next part to the talk is where things get weird. She goes on to mention that once the background check is cleared I can be given a start date from one day after, up to 2 months. 2 months? In my mind I wondered if I heard her right. When I didn't respond she asked if I still would like to consider the position. I respond that if the start date is near the point of being contacted I'd accept but if it's 2 months out I wouldn't. She then stated they'd need a Yes or No from me. I respond with a, "Yes we'll see what happens." After a few back and forth sentences we hang up. I was thinking the whole time throughout the talk and a few seconds after the call ended I knew what I needed to do. I called the recruiter back and the line went to voicemail. A minute later she returns the call. I let her know my decision to withdraw my acceptance, and why. When done talking I reflected a bit more. Something didn't seem right about the situation. In all of my work history I have never went through or heard anyone be told that they may be given a start date upon contact of 1 day up to 2 months.

After speaking to a Human Resources manager within my LinkedIn network, and confirming that this was unusual I decided to contact who was in charge of human resources, along with whoever is in charge of operations. I compose an email with both of their email addresses attached so they're both aware it's a mass email.

While researching who to contact I take the time to look over the executive team, and middle management. I see not one person of African descent and mainly see Caucasians. I was already aware that the Department of Fair Employment & Housing in California stepped in and filed a law suit against Tesla on behalf of Black workers who accused the company of racism for years. For a government agency to step in there has to be hard proof. In light of this I considered the circumstances around my interview, and recruiting experience as well as the environment. There are only 7.6% people of African descent in Austin. 34% Hispanic Latino, 7% Asian, and 48.9% Anglo (non-Hispanic White.) All together Austin is close to 70% White includes White Latinos, Anglo-Saxon, Christian; etc. Austin has a lot of racist history concerning African Americans in the past, and now with the gentrification of the East side of the city which used to be predominantly Black owned. The majority of the Spanish speaking community in Austin is Mexican and they're extremely racist as the majority are White Hispanic. In their mother nation they're lineage ties to the Spaniards of Europe who enslaved the indigenous populations in Mexico and Central America. They're basically Europeans who speak Spanish who for some reason get classified in the U.S. as being minority. In Latin countries the light skinned population is of the ruling class and are extremely biased toward the darker skinned population. They've brought, and continue to bring their Eurocentric ideals across the Mexican border into the U.S. I've worked in construction, and many labor environments where I've dealt with them daily. Being a person who's very situational aware, and has a deeper understanding of social behavior than most people I have a keen eye to things which most people don't acknowledge. The woman who called me for the initial interview via the web was Latino, and so was the woman who called me a few days after the drug screen test. I heard the male laugh in the background when she mentioned the 2 month wait and I knew then there was some extra nonsense going on. The exact thoughts which came to mind were, "Here we go with this Latino White people nonsense."

My experience in Austin is that White people desire Black men to be gay, or Lgbt. If religious they want them to be Christian. They would prefer them to be from Austin, or some other TX city. This is because, straight Black men are masculine by nature and less inclined to deal with nonsense. Non-Christian Black men accept less nonsense. The North East states and West coast are different cultural environments where Black people are a lot more progressive and organized. It's all about control. In regards to Latinos. Texas is connected to the Mexican border and was once a part of Mexico. For them the Black population represents a threat to their progress and stability because Texas is one of the few states that they organized politically in. Although they've relied on Black leadership and social programs in the past, and still do rely on Blacks. By no means are they truly with Black people in solidarity. As a middle aged man I've seen many cities, states, worked in different industries and have been around all kinds of people from different social, and economic backgrounds so I decipher what's truth from what's represented in dialogue. It was clear to me that these two women were going to be gate keepers to ensure Latinos get into positions at Tesla over other minorities. I've had enough experiences with life and my senses to know what I know and be secure in the knowing.

The situation reminded me of how important it is to think at your highest, and sometimes not match frequencies. This is why I chose to send an email to the higher ups. Considering Tesla history in regards to experience with Black people I knew I wouldn't receive a response. Yet I wanted to make the higher ups aware of what practices were taking place at the recruiter level, and I was aware that the process seemed a bit bias and sketchy. Tesla was placing workers currently within the Giga factory, and no one I spoke to mentioned anything about a possible 2 month wait time. In fact they all were surprised and bewildered when I told them what I was told and asked. I emailed to find out if this recruiter's behavior was customary to the Tesla recruiting process. I knew it wasn't and I was sure I wasn't going to receive an email back from anyone. I didn't receive a response either. Writing my experience in this book is enough because it puts others on notice to be awake and aware.

The experience further validated my belief that not every opportunity is the right opportunity for you. It's important to also have a level of respect and expectation for yourself as to what you will allow from others. The fact the guy was laughing in the background when the recruiter mentioned two months told me they had me figured out wrong.

Everything's An Equation and Pattern

Through watching and analyzing I've begun to understand that every act from the smallest to the largest is an equation. Whether this act is thought or physical behavior the same rule applies. Since everything is the sum of Cause and Effect all things are the result of a previous thought and act, and this creates a pattern. Mathematics is the only precise science known to man and when one views things in this light they'll begin to see how all events form and take shape. In this they'll see a pattern. When we do this we can go back and modify thoughts, behaviors to produce more favorable outcomes.

I haven't been the greatest seer with predicting the outcome of my own thoughts and behaviors and what would be the effects. On the contrary though I've been able to look at others and pretty much predict with accuracy the blossoming of greatness, as well as stature of mediocrity, or the work of self-killing. Yes, I say self-killing because many create the thoughts and actions which produce their downfall. Just as we produce the thoughts and actions which move us to achievement of the things which enrich our lives and bring satisfaction.

Today more than ever I'm aware of the power I have over events in my life even amongst outside forces which seek to sway me into negative thoughts and behavioral patterns. I've learned how to remove myself from people and environments when I receive vibes that present a sense of anxiety or frustration. I just don't need to be involved, and I don't have to regardless of what others think. We live in a society where being weak-minded and boned is normal so people are accepting of people's nonsense. I'm no ones psychologist, or enabler when it comes to anything that's of detriment of me; especially my mental health. Respecting yourself and making yourself a priority is self-care, and it's something we all should be aware of and make a priority. Without YOU nothing in your life happens!

I've learned to be aware when people are striving to push my buttons to obtain a reaction. I'm not a video game, machine, or anything of alignment with anyone's immaturity or mental illness. The next person's issues are separate from myself and since this is so I'm always aware of what I can do. The first thing which comes to mind is that in most instances I can always remove myself, or limit my interaction.

Right before Covid19 hit I had an assignment for an employment agency operating a buck hoist at a construction site in Austin, TX. If you're not familiar with what a buck hoist is to be simple about it lets just say it's an elevator on the outside of a multi-level construction building being erected. It's used to bring freight and workers to each floor. There were two on the site, and I operated one and the other was operated by a young lady.

On a construction site the workers consist of the general contractors company. They're the ones overseeing the project and then workers belonging to the different contractor companies contracted by the general contracting company to provide services such as plumbing, lighting, framing, sheetrock, roofing, tiling, cement work; etc. The bigger the building project the more companies involved.

The workers belonging to the general contractor mainly were Caucasian except for the foreman and his team who were Latino. Well let's say Mexican because in Texas most of the Spanish speaking population are of Mexican descent, with a minority mixture of Central American nations.

The supervisor of the general contractor company picked the young lady I was working with himself. She ran the buck hoist on a previous building his company constructed. I worked with her at a previous assignment and she put me on to this job. She also let me know that the foreman really didn't want a Black person running the buck hoist. He wanted one of his own kind (Mexican) but had no say in the matter because the sites GC put who he wanted there.

As time went by I learned for myself just by paying attention that the foreman was indeed one who preferred working and dealing with his own kind. I could tell that he and some of the others didn't really care for me. It mainly had to do with me not taking anyone's nonsense than it did with being African American. They wanted someone they could push around, and I'm no softie so they couldn't influence me to do things which went outside the protocol. It was their desire to get me to leave on my own so they wouldn't have issues with the project GC.

On construction sites they use wooden platforms to construct the level of flooring so they can lay down mesh wiring and the foundation to pore in cement. Each platform connects and locks into the other with large keys. I don't know how much these keys weigh. I would say 4lbs, maybe less or more. The first time from around the 9th floor a ring of three keys fell all the way down hitting the top of the buck hoist. A loud clank sound echoed. One things for sure if it hit someone on their hard hat it could possibly knock them out, or down to the ground. If it hit them in their body, bones could be broken or possibly worse. The first time it happened I didn't think it was a mistake because it happened working overtime after hours when all of the general contractor office had left. By this time I was there now for about 90 days and this never happened before. Now all of the sudden such a big mistake doing overtime again the keys drop but this time about 10ft away from the buck hoist to the ground and I was walking around not too far from the area. I knew then that I was going to be put in a situation sooner or later that I was going to have to hurt one of them guys. I was also having some friction with the foreman about putting more people in the buck hoist than the city of Austin mandated per Covid guidelines. I believe it was the buck hoist operator plus

4 occupants. He kept putting his whole team which was about seven inside. I knew this was probably part of an elaborate scheme or plan they were doing in cooperation to get me to leave, but I didn't care. Life has taught me a lot and in youth I was a different person and coming into the late 40's brought me to a different state of manhood as well. Bad vibes, bad energy, confrontational environments and all that surrounds such aren't worth my time. They weren't taking anything from me. It was a temporary job, temporary placement, and an opportunity for me to take what I can get for a period of time and keep it moving. I took advantage of the opportunity and was saving money as I knew it wouldn't last forever. Now was the time to move on and I was going to. Predicting outcomes and seeing the beginnings of patterns is so important so one can adjust properly.

The general contractor was on vacation and when he came back text me asking why I left. I told him it was best that I left for myself and him because I was going to get into it with one of them guys. I didn't state any of the issues but he was aware of the racial geopolitical issues and aware that the Mexicans were a bit of trouble. He actually warned me one day indirectly mentioning to make sure they weren't giving the buck hoist operator next to me a hard time. A few times I had to address a few of them that she kicked out her buck hoist and wouldn't give rides up. Not all of them were an issue because most of them were cordial but there were enough of them who were characters.

I read the equation and recognized the pattern which was going to lead to an unfavorable situation for me. People who have nothing to lose will help you lose everything, and I couldn't just stand back and let this happen.

Intuition and psyche are tools to steer you clear of unfavorable circumstances, and also a road map to favorable travels. It's very important to pay attention to yourself. It's for your own good.

There's Not a More Prized As-set than Your-self

Throughout the Third Eye Awakening series I've mentioned many times the value of oneself. Here I hope to be able to clarify through a different angle. All of the learning, travels, obstacles, wins, losses, and lessons are all dependent upon the value you place upon yourself. The more credit you give yourself for your outcomes the more responsibility you will take for your thoughts, actions and outcomes. All of this comes with the realization that you alone have the most effect on your life when you realize your power.

Your Intuition and Psyche when your realization of self is of abundance serves as a GPS and guide to manifest best outcomes. When you're not in tune the opposite is obtained because you become a tool to produce for others. The point is you will either serve your highest good or that of others. The free man and the slave both serve, and have a purpose. Perception is everything. Great people are useful, but the point is not to be used. There's the difference.

As a young man, more like teen because I was around 15 at the time. I thought about how people work 40 to 45 years of their life to collect a social security check. A social security check which will not be equal to the cost of living and so many of them end up working into their 60's and beyond. This is nothing but economic slavery. Even at 15 years old I saw it was predatory and ridiculous. Actually this is one of the factors which drove me to the fast life of the streets. But this is another book. Survivor I Changed the Rules the first book of my autobiography series explains the details of my street adventures and why.

Without you there's No Story

Everyone has a book of life and the details are being written every second of the day. Without you there's no story. You're the main character, star and driving force to the experience. Every relationship you establish and encounter is dependent upon you. It's your story, and all the possibilities and happenings are a direct result of you.

We were created in thought and experience, and therefore we are thought and experience. There's a saying which implies that 'Man is mind." I'm assuming that the meaning behind this is that the depth of ones intellect is their foundation to what's possible.

Let me tell you a personal story. As a person who is drug and alcohol free even before I understood how important it was to ones state of mind to be free of substances I understood that I was my most valuable asset. Now at 51 years old and on this very day which is my birthday I'm looking back over the years and experiences realizing that money accomplishments and nothing external has ever held more value than my being and what I've been able to infuse within myself. Enlightenment whether it be through learning or experiencing has helped me through the good and bad in more ways than anything else has. The last decade I had to basically start over in every area of my life from ground zero. I really don't think that many people could have handled the experience without turning to drugs, alcohol, or even both. I handled it all with the mentality that it could get worse, and it could be worse. The reality that others lives are worse than mine never got lost on me, and never will. It doesn't mean there weren't days, weeks and even months where I wasn't sad or depressed because there were them moments. I just went within, counseled myself and moved past them moments. There's a vision I hold in my mind of myself and it's grand, and I'm walking and reaching forth to dwell in it, and you should too.

I believe the hardest part of the last decade was the first three years. I would say 2010-2013 because I was in shock and denial about my situation and all that it meant. I no longer had national distribution for my books. I had just got out of arbitration with the new distributor which took over publisher contracts and who I refused to do business with. Amazon invention of eBooks had slowed down paperback book sales considerably. I didn't have the cash to print high volume print runs like I was doing before because of slow sales, along with one year loss of chain retail book sales. I let go of about 2,000 books in the new distributors' warehouse inventory. Financially I was hurt and just getting by. Around 2014 I truly came to terms with my situation and made the commitment to learn all the things I needed to learn to figure out why the things went the way they did, and how I could be prepared for the future. I realized there were things I needed to learn and work on concerning myself. If you're going through a loss from my experience I would say to acknowledge the loss, mourn and evaluate.

It's 2022 and through the whole process of this latest awakening along with my growth has been the removal of a lot of thoughts, behaviors and even people which were weighing me down. Some friends and family winded up getting the axe or being put in a zone where the level of contact is befitting for the type of relationship we have. It kind of reminds me of when I came home in 2000 from doing a 2 year parole violation and I realized if I was going to change my life I would have to change environments and associations. I did this and within four years of starting an entry level position, and four jobs later I winded up in a management position. Evolving requires many things, and the letting go of things which don't serve your greater good is one of them.

It's a tragedy but necessary at the same time. Through our emotions, hurt and pain is the way to logic and doing what's necessary. Money can't get you there. Attachment to social status, the need to be liked can't get you there neither. Only the realization that you're your most important asset. You need to think and move in this energy and life will align you with all that supports the greater good for you.

I've had dreams and also visions while awake which have shown me the true nature of my relationships and situations. Many times I've chosen to ignore or not believe. Yet life has always brought me to the path to see for myself the reality forcing me to accept what is true. In the end I've been forced to acknowledge that if I don't recognize there's only Self and everything else is a given I couldn't free myself. Every reality is of the mind first before we actualize it in our world.

Our nature is to be free from the need of attachments. Even when we create children they're their own lives which we have no ownership rights. We nurture them to evolve into their own consciousness and reality. We betray ourselves when we don't believe ourselves when the vision in our mind is showing us as plain as day what things are regardless what we think should be.

R&D: Research & Development

When one hears the term research and development one thinks of product development, laboratories, companies, and organizations. R&D can also apply to one's life. If you're seeking a job you may look at your skills, resume, and research job boards then shop your resume and see where you stand in the job market according to positions and pay. From this point you may decide to upgrade your skills according to what you find out from the data.

With the goals I seek to achieve in life as I ponder and meditate daily the vision came to me of the things I would need to learn through study. It was obvious I was going to need to test the waters and try many different things in regards to action. I started taking online courses in business, marketing, thought leadership and also tried different strategies with social media marketing. With my books I realized that I was going to have to develop an all around program broader than just face to face, and business to customer sales. I'm not going to give my personal process away because what works and is for me is for me, and most importantly the publishing program I'm working & fine tuning is for Therone Shellman Media not for anyone else's company. Can't give the company secrets away. I think the point is understood though. Every area of your life you must research and develop a process to do things that not just works for you but also produces great results.

Coming back to NY In the summer of 2022 I decided to stay in Queens at a private hotel which is more like an extended stay. Every room has a refrigerator and desk along with bed, and they provide snacks and other amenities. There's 3 rooms, and most of the time there's maybe one other occupant. Sitting at my desk I'm thinking and setting in my mind that over the next three-four weeks I need to be finished with the first draft of Third Eye Awakening V so the book can be published in November. Working on the manuscript daily I began visualizing month to month objectives. In fact I started writing them down for more sure measure. The different areas of my life are like a fragmented puzzle but everything I've been doing coincides with my goals. One of these goals being my book publishing objectives. Now that I'm situating everything I realize that what I've done is no different than an experiment or case study to produce a determined objective. You as well can do this in your life. Be

more methodical about your objectives
and also the different areas in your life.
Utilize your psyche to see the different el-
ements and individual puzzle pieces and
your ultimate goal. This means that everything you do must benefit putting the
puzzle together which is your ultimate
goal. I believe that if people viewed their
life in this manner they would be more
thoughtful and careful with the decisions
they make in every area of their life. If one
is seeking an outcome and realizes that
they have the power to effect outcomes
most of the time. Why wouldn't they
change what they're doing? It would be
senseless not to after all time and effort is
valuable. Everyone desires to win even if
they're scared too. I've known fear and
boldness most of my life. Having only you
to rely on can be frightening when you
first accept the reality. I'm a logical person
and I accepted reality and it's pushed me
to move when I need to. It's me or nothing
happens.

Let me tell you another quick little personal story. Over the last two years since the
start of Covid I've been working as an independent contractor through a few apps.
I believe that working doesn't only provide
income but it's also a way to develop

skills. Being on the topic of Research & Development and the book being about Intuition and Psyche I'm reminded of why I even started on this path. I envision myself owning retail stores, warehouses, and businesses within many industries. I was basically pushed into pursuing this opportunity because of the setbacks with Covid. The setback for me was really a setup to prepare me for the future. "It's a marathon not a sprint" is a saying I all of the sudden started dreaming and thinking about. I would work at some places and pay attention to the organizations processes, the good and the bad. Most importantly I began to think about how I would and am going to do things.

The basis of all final decisions are the result of discovery and discovery comes from trying different methods & visualization. Visualization is the unseen hand nudging and prodding one to move here and there to try this and that; etc.

Era of Gang Stalkers

In a forth coming book titled 'Street Knowledge' I will speak about an associate turned police informant, and how I had become a target of gang stalking and a campaign smear because I wouldn't participate in the program being run in his home town of Bellport, NY by the Suffolk County Police Department.

My issues with gang stalking and being profiled are not isolated from others like myself. I believe that if you're a Black man with affiliations with organizations which fall outside the scope of traditional American teachings then you're a prime candidate to be under surveillance once you're found out. The same can be said of Caucasian Americans or anyone else but not as such a high degree as people of African descent. As J Edgar Hoover put it Black Empowerment is America's number one threat. The reason is obvious. This country was built upon the slavery, disenfranchisement and stealing of physical labor and mental resources of Black Americans and yet they've still failed to pay reparations. In my moral compass I would always fear someone or a group of people I did this to. So it's obvious why White leadership in this nation has a fixation with targeting Black populations. Law enforcement organizations, fraternal, civic, community networks and spiritual based organizations are known to utilize their network to target people through gang stalking activity. The first program was established by J. Edgar Hoover called COINTEL.

For anyone who's a victim of online gang stalking, take pictures (screen shots), and obtain as much as info about the subjects as possible. You can file a case on the following government website IC3.gov/ There's no established government agency as of now which specifically handles gang stalking activities.

If you feel you're being stalked by members of government, fraternal or civic organizations off the internet and in the world take pictures, obtain as much info as possible and bring in person, or send via the mail to your state attorney general. I would recommend that you send certified mail sign return receipt.

Intimidation Tactic

Gang stalking is often utilized as a way of intimidation and silencing by groups of people and organizations. This tactic is very old, but has become more socially aware due to social media and how easy communication can reach people. In the past a person would just be considered paranoid, but now with so many people over the years who have come out against government agencies, employers, industry leaders, law enforcement, civic and religious organization members, and private citizens the public is on full alert to how real the threat of gang stalking is. In most cases the desired result is silence, suicide, murder, or for the person to do something to jeopardize their freedom and get incarcerated. In Street Knowledge the friend turned associate and Judas I'm going to speak on was trying to instigate a situation so I could react do something to someone and catch a case. They (him, his associates and his police buddies in the 5th precinct in Suffolk County, N.Y.) wanted me out the way. It just didn't work out the way they planned because my intuition is very strong.

The first story is about a young lady who had become an assistant district attorney in Suffolk County, NY. I knew her going back to the 1990's. We hung out sometimes, which was mostly at a friend's house. I need to mention she's Caucasian because this is very important to the story. Her friend was Black. This young Caucasian lady was into Black guys, and this is also important to the story.

Did we ever mess around like sleep with one another, or kiss? No, she was a bit immature and I've never been into goofiness so I basically would come around and hang out with them laugh, joke, chill for a little while and go about my business. It never got serious though.

I was in the street hustling doing my thing, and also on parole. I believe through two of my parole violations we kept in contact. So we never got serious but remained cool. Cool enough though for her to take the time to write me while in prison. She was away in law school while I was doing a parole violation in 1997. I came home and we lost contact. I saw her once again when she came home for school break around 2001. I remember this because I had just gotten released from parole and bought my first car a 1990 Honda Accord Coupe. Every now and then we spoke on the phone but within a matter of a few years we went back to our own lives. I was in NY, and she was in the Midwest.

Around 2009 I began setting up with my books at a small take out restaurant called Spicy's known for its fried chicken in Bellport, NY (Long Island.) We reconnected on the internet and by now she had graduated law school taking a job at the district attorney's office. Needless to say being a Black man who has experienced the sting of racism and White supremacy my whole life, being vocal about my stance and thinking didn't sit well with the White girl who was now mingling amongst her White co-workers who in most cases came from a totally different background than her. She hang around more with Black kids in school than her own kind. Now having gone to college for several years, working in the district attorney's office, she was finding her placing amongst her peers who were now mainly White. Suffolk County is run by liberals. Notably along with Nassau County, Long Island between the two counties is known as one of the most segregated communities in the country and racist. Not the down south type of 'nigger' in your face racism found in many conservative districts but the systematic racism that liberals have come to master. The

Suffolk County Police department and courts have one of the highest conviction rates in the nation. People have tried for many years to sue Riverhead County jail for its mistreatment of prisoners, and unhealthy living conditions. Without success because the rumor is Long island lawyers will not take the case. From the sheriff's department to law enforcement and the courts everyone's related. From personal experience I do know how corrupt law enforcement and the courts are. I received a 4to12 year prison sentence under an illegal conviction. My case never went to a grand jury hearing which is a NYS mandate to obtain an indictment. Instead they utilized a false accusatory instrument and my court appointed attorney along with judge went along with it.

Well let's get back to the story. She and I began getting into debates on one of the social media platforms. I'm straightforward so if you get into a debate with me you better know your stuff and have a good sense of emotional intelligence or you're going to get into your feelings. After a while of doing this which was her mostly trying to challenge my posts and me basically beating her up with researched information she began to get into her feelings. Next thing I know I begin to get a bunch of spam posts from Caucasian women. Every time I posted anything concerning Black history or social issues someone would come with a spam comment. It was obvious as to why it was happening. I had now become a target, and possibly even employees from the Suffolk County District Attorney's Office was in on it. I also knew that I was being followed. Whenever I went to the Patchogue library I s I was being profiled and by this time two of my social media profiles were being spammed regularly. I made the decision to stop utilizing the profiles altogether and created Therone Shellman Media profiles, and for about six months I stopped social media activity. When I returned back to social media I began utilizing a few other social media sites and I was still being spammed. Now the sites had created the block feature and so instead of responding to comments I began blocking profiles. After a while the comments stopped. I moved away from the Suffolk County area, and out of state to do business. Being out of site, it also took me out of mind.

Over the years she created a few profiles outside her name, and on one of the other sites would respond to my posts in agreement. I was fully unbothered and responded in kind. After a couple of tries she was aware that our association was over and going to remain this way. She stopped commenting to my posts, and for which I was more than glad because the association was over.

Life Will Teach You & Aide You with Developing Necessary Tools

I spent many of the late teen years and 20's incarcerated or in the streets selling drugs sticking up drug dealers; etc. The life I lived out of necessity caused me to become very situational aware of any environment I encounter. My thinking is to have eyesight of at least 1 block to 1 ½ blocks ahead 20-30ft on each side of you, and as you move forward always be aware of your back. You should be able to hear 15-20ft behind you. The majority of people you can walk right up on them without them being aware until the last few seconds. As I walk out in public I'm always scanning people within the 10ft range, paying attention to where they're hands are, where their eyes are focused at, taking in their energy and vibrations.

In the first book to my autobiography series Survivor I Changed the Rules I reveal a fraction of my life. The fact remains I've not lived an ordinary life and because of this I had to learn many things the average person doesn't feel the need to to be able to survive. I'm going to tell you a few stories that are in line with the subject of gang stalking. I'm sure I've had other experiences but the first experience where I was fully aware of the happening would be dealing with the U.S. Army.

Beginning around 2012 I had become a short term vendor with AAFES (Army Air Force Exchange Services.) From 1-4 weeks at a time I would set up at a kiosk with the APEX which is a mall situated on an Army of Air Force base. At the time I was selling scented oils, incense, shea butter, lotions, soaps and my book titles periodically.

I noticed I was being followed while in Killeen, TX and Fort Hood area. Even on the base I was being watched. Of course there are necessary security measures but I can tell there was more going on and I was actually being profiled to the point of being stalked. My street knowledge and awareness naturally kicked in and I began to pay attention. After about a few months of setting up on the base I had developed a good customer base. Many of them would stop by to talk politics, world events and Black issues. One of the soldiers who I knew was aware of the happenings on the base because what he was into made it necessary to move around the different organizations on the base. I told him that I was being followed around. He mentioned that someone told him that I was under some type of investigation but the details as to why weren't known. He wasn't shy in admitting that the military is racist and me being a Black man and having the type of political and social views that have caused me to stand out. On top of this I was steadily building a customer base of Black customers, many of them young soldiers.

We didn't discuss the matter again, and I saw him whenever I set up, and he always supported and bought products. For good reason I remained watchful. I could tell there were unseen forces who were striving to push me out. Every now and then issues would arise like vendor dates being cancelled, or me being placed at a kiosk which was in a bad location inside the APEX (mall.)

I could tell over the years they were trying to push me out. I winded up applying to set up at Fort Carlisle Barracks in Pennsylvania around 2015 and I was denied access by the Commander there on the grounds of my past criminal record. A felony conviction of robbery dating back to 1990 when I was seventeen years old. My intuition told me it was more to this because Carlisle and the surrounding community is basically Caucasian, and the base itself doesn't have a huge Black population. The fact the Army trains people to kill every day, 365 days of the year and he's questioning my morals and values, past and present life to me was a bit humorous. It made no sense actually because at the time of my application I had no other felony misdemeanor convictions for over the decades. In 2020 I strived to gain access to Fort Hood Army base and was denied access on the grounds of the Fort Hood Carlisle situation. I appealed and won, and when I strived to come to Fort Hamilton in Brooklyn when I came back to NY I was again denied access even though I had copies of my appeal being granted, and it specifically stating access to Army bases for the purpose of work was reinstated. At the visitor center I was once again handed an access denied packet with paperwork to appeal. It's obvious I was being targeted, and the cause was greater than my 30 year old felony conviction. The fact is there are gang members, militia members, White supremacists, rapists, murderers and many other kinds of delinquents on Army bases but I was being singled out because of a past conviction. Meanwhile most of all the killings, rapes, assaults have been done by enlisted, or retired soldiers. There was something deeper to this. When I left Fort Hamilton visitor center that day I noticed I was being profiled and followed by a young woman. I got on the bus and she got on, and I winded up seeing her 4 or 5 times after that day in different parts of NYC. Coincidence? No not at all.

Not Quite Done

You thought I was done with you but I'm not. In fact I have one last story. A few years ago I decide to come back to NY from down south for a while. My main purpose was to sell 400-500 books and to concentrate on the 4 books of the Third Eye Awakening series along with All You

Need to Know to Become an Entrepreneur and The Secrets of Self-Publishing 2.

I check into a hotel as soon as I arrive realizing that most of my activity is going to take place in Queens, Brooklyn and Manhattan. I decide logistically it would be best to stay in Queens as opposed to Long Island. Hotels are expensive and so I realize paying $1800 a month would be steep and burn through my financial resources. The time isn't 2005-2010 where the street market is booming. In them years I was selling 10-30 books a day whenever I stepped out. Covid changed the economic landscape and so it would be urgent for me to be watchful and frugal with my money. I stayed at the hotel for one month and by the third week I found a room to rent in Saint Albans which is right next to Jamaica, NY. I knew I was only going to be in New York for 4 to 5 months so it wouldn't make sense to find an apartment. Plus I didn't want to spend more than $1,000 a month. A studio would run around $1400-$1600.

The Saint Albans area I moved to consisted of mainly Central American Latinos and Black Caribbean. I stood out like a saw thumb as it was obvious I'm a Foundational Black American by the clothes I wore. So they watched my every move, and I watched them as well. People who migrate into the U.S. tend to have negative views of Black Americans. The movies and media has something to do with this as well rumors spread through the immigration process. Marcus Garvey was from Jamaica and he was a fierce advocate of Pan Africanism which is the idea that Black people globally are one and share the same goal for empowerment. Those Caribbean's who know of him and others like him tend to be cool and quite different than those brainwashed by British and French teachings and education. The fact is all melinated people who come to the U.S. do so because of the struggles Foundational Black Americans have made. If they're not from Eastern Europe most White Americans don't want them to have immigration access. Back to my story. Aside from being an author and other things I'm also a good salesman and so I'm always looking for areas and locations where I can sell my books at. I found an area where there was a deli and a bus stop very near and it was also within a residential area but yet had a good amount of foot traffic. I sold about 17 books the first day, and had some very interesting talks in regards to self-development as it relates to self and the Black community. I also noticed I was being watched. I ran into a female author, and it turns out her boyfriend and some authors are also published through her company. It was obvious they didn't have much success because they weren't out and about with the books, and people in the neighborhood didn't know their work. Yet, I could sense from the boyfriend a bit of jealousy and there were some others who I could tell were apart of their circle. I'm no newbie to the streets and I've been around many environments dealing with all types of people so I read and picked up on the vibes very quickly. I wind up setting up at that location one more time before deciding to move around the city. I learned very quickly them two were trying to become cool with me so they could basically utilize my platform and hustle to sell their books. Their catalog mainly consisted of street stories and works which are totally the opposite of what my program is about. My works are all about enlightenment, self-development and aspects of business. Most importantly I was spending $0 marketing, and 99% of sales were the result of hand to hand sales. Whether this be vendor events, street sales or another medium where I came in contact with customers face to face. Everything I was doing they could have been doing too but they weren't because it's hard work, and many people want others to do their work for them. I wasn't going to do their work, and I wasn't going to affiliate with them beyond being cordial. I'm sure they realized I was on to them and wasn't falling for any part of the nonsense. Although they live in the same communities the different factions in the Caribbean community have no reservations about scamming each other, and as an outsider I knew to pay attention. Most of the community are hard working people who live honest lives, but as with most of the world there are the people who scheme and scam their way through opportunities and life. The area is a pretty tight knit community and so I knew I was being watched when I left and also when I would arrive. As an outsider I'm sure they were trying to figure out how they could scam me, and get over but I wasn't there to get familiar with anyone and I treated the environment as a temporary place to lay my head. I would go to a few of the convenience stores, the laundromat, a few food take outs, a Chinese place and that was it. There was also a little store called RBG (which stands for Red, Black, and Green. These are the colors of the Black

Liberation flag) owned by two Black men where I would buy ginger ale, root beer soda from. Other than this I was in and out, and I moved like this for the 4 months I was back in NY. I worked the whole time and winded up dedicating 1-3 days to selling books. I believe I reached my goal of 400 books but winded up leaving to go back down south with about 140 books.

End In Mind:

It's no wonder why I've held an interest in writing books. The process requires visualization and if not having an end in mind, at least having a desire to journey down a specific course. Visualization is what fuels the journey. Authoring a book is like putting a puzzle together. For most of my books I started with composing a synopsis. A synopsis a 3-4 paragraph mini outline of the important messaging in the book. It's a guideline as to what the books about. If you've ever purchased a puzzle you'll notice that although the box comes with many loose pieces there's a picture of the completed puzzle. In most cases it's on the front of the box, and usually there's an insert with a picture of the completed puzzle as well. In your mind is now a picture of how those many loose pieces are supposed to come together and look. Some puzzles come with hundreds of loose pieces, and the idea of putting it all together is enough to give anxiety because it's hard not to get anxious. Well, at least for me anyway. Puzzles, writing in its various forms, and any building exercises are great for developing visualization. It just occurred to me that survival tactics are also great for building visualization. When I was in the streets as a younger man living the street hustler life it was necessary that I stayed mentally sharp and aware. I paid attention to everything, the people, car, noises and even vibes. Yes I did say vibes. Everything at its most infinite existence is vibrations in survival made the nature of you kicks in.

This is a hard pill to swallow but a necessary one. Probably the most important aspect of visualization and psyche is to be able to look within self and with honesty. I pondered this idea for quite a while, and it was hard to accept but I did because I had no choice but to. I realized that at our core humans are vile creatures. We can come together and build cities and nations, and we can also come together to plunder, murder and destroy and find justification. Ones greatest supporter can also become an enemy within a matter of just one choice. It's just this simple.

With all gloom, doom and hardships that we see around us and maybe even in our own lives perhaps the gift and power of visualization and our psyche is to picture the best possible state and outcome for the world and our own personal lives and remain fixed in this vision whatever that looks like because if we can see it, and believe it then we can move toward and work for it. In my personal life this is where I'm at and I know there are those who wish other than this because they profit from human dysfunction but I'm all in and am committed to being at opposition to ideas and those who hold dear to ideas and behaviors which threaten our social equality as individuals and a global society.

As crazy as this may seem the truth is mankind is an enemy of knowledge because with knowledge comes the understanding of principles of what's right and what's wrong based on the ideas and actions which build as opposed to those which are destructive. Right becomes wrong and wrong becomes right when sensationalism, opinions, and corruption run rampant like the plague. The very idea of thinking and thinking in an independent manner becomes a threat and enemy to the program most of society and the powers that be are running on. Under this environment visualization and self-realization aren't promoted or championed as behavior for the Individual. Yet, it's necessary because the heights a nation can rise is dependent upon the heights its people can rise in mind.

Last Thoughts:
Through all the treachery, backstabbing, lying and everything else I've experienced one thing remains certain and this is that my faith is unbreakable and my desire to keep living, writing and expressing my ideals will not be stopped. I also believe in karma and a natural spiritual order that is beyond the desires of man & which many of the old world values and morals for man were shaped. Many of such principles can be found in spiritual texts. The 42 Principles of Ma 'at are an example. As a child and teen I was always told by adults that I was smart and that I should be a leader, or that one day I would be important. As they say people can see you better than you see themselves. I believe that many of the struggles I've faced have been to prepare and build me into the person I need to be. I also believe that people forming against me from childhood to adulthood had and has something to do with what they see in me. I've never been a person to follow what everyone else is doing or feel the need to explain myself as to why not and so because of this I've stood out. When I began writing and published my first novel Love Don't Live Here I became vocal about my views on race matters, politics, spirituality and the first group of people I had is-

sues with were Black people in the literary industry. My views is that artists in some way have an obligation to be some form of upliftment and this is especially so for Black artists. To use your platform as a way to just entertain and miseducate people is a disservice. I'm a conscious literary, audio, visual artist and creative and for this I was opposed by many Black writers and literary professionals who saw no responsibility and only wanted to make money and thought my messaging was an issue. The crazy thing now is that it's a decade later and many of these folks are on some Black Power stuff when they weren't about any of this before. The second group of people who I came into issue with were White supremacists hiding behind the Catholic faith. They didn't like the fact that I'm a Black man whose aware of his history and lineage. Black people were the first people, and so they brought civilization, education and the knowledge of all the sciences and spirituality to the planet earth. This is truth, but it doesn't sit well with White supremacists and those who use Christianity or Catholism as a shield for their dirty ways. So they started attacking my business in various ways since they couldn't tempt me into become an intellectually passive Negro. One of my titles The

Secrets of Self-Publishing had a review where the review gave a poor review, and actually mentioned they were Catholic in the review. Now what does religion have to do with self-publishing? Nothing at all. The person who reviewed under a fake name just wanted me to know that was some sort of attack against my personal and spiritual views which I was posting on Myspace because this was the social media platform which I mainly utilized at the time. A few years later the review was re-moved by Amazon after I had questioned another review and asked them to investigate. There's been a concerted effort to stop me from writing and publishing books because of my ideas, and it hasn't just been one group, or race either. As a person who has a strong belief in the nature of things such as a woman was made for man and man for woman, and that food essentially is what comes from the earth, and manmade things such as drugs and liquor which take us out of our natural thinking are detrimental I'm not in line with the general ideas and way of life which have made its way into mainstream society. These are just some of the views of mine which strike a nerve with some people and so we stand on separate sides of the fence, and they would like to silence me. But I won't be silenced by anyone on anything which is important to me. Unlike many people who go to religious houses of worship certain days of the week and are conscious of the ideas of their faith for that moment my faith is engrained in my lifestyle and way of life and I live it 24/7. I may fall short here and there but I make a conscious effort to readjust and get back on track. Gang stalking is an action by the weak to come together to attack someone who they're scared of and intimidated by. The person is more than they are as individuals and in many ways even as a group. We are constantly at war with ourselves and at war with others and it's our experiences which enable us to see where we stand and are navigating toward. I've possessed way more money in my life at many points throughout my life. Yet I've never been as well equipped mentally with knowledge and skills than I am now. Now it's like I'm really out of school and ready to deal with the world, and it's my hope that you to get to this point in your life. I'm excited, and ready to complete the many things I started and had to leave alone for a bit. I'm also ready to do all the other things that I want to do. Hopefully this work has been an enjoyment to ready and provided some bit of insight into your own struggles and path.